# THE CHAOS AND THE PROFIT

## STRATEGIC APPROACH TO SUPERIOR PERFORMANCE IN DIFFICULT TIMES

# THE CHAOS AND THE PROFIT

## STRATEGIC APPROACH TO SUPERIOR PERFORMANCE IN DIFFICULT TIMES

### BRIAN REUBEN

*Swift Publishing*

Copyright © 2020 by Brian O. Reuben.
All rights reserved.
Published by Swift Publishing

No part of this publication may be reproduced, stored in a retrieval system, or transmitted in any form or by any means, electronic, mechanical, photocopying, recording, scanning, or otherwise, except with Author's express permission.

Requests to the Author for permission should be addressed to: drbrianreuben@icloud.com

Limit of Liability/Disclaimer of Warranty: While the publisher and author have used their best efforts in preparing this book, they make no representations or warranties with respect to the accuracy or completeness of the contents of this book and specifically disclaim any implied warranties of merchantability or fitness for a particular purpose. No warranty may be created or extended by sales representatives or written sales materials. The advice and strategies contained herein may not be suitable for your situation. You should consult with a professional where appropriate. Neither the publisher nor the author shall be liable for any loss of profit or other commercial damages, including but not limited to special, incidental, consequential, or other damages.

ISBN-13: 9798562903884
ISBN: 8562903884

Printed in the United States of America.

To Sunesis, Darryl and Bliss

Being successful is not just about being busy, it is being about the right things. Activities that don't add up to the intended value is meaningless and a waste of effort. This means that companies incur losses or make profit at the activity level. Strategic gains are made at activity level not when the products are sold.

- Dr Brian Reuben

# CONTENTS

| | | |
|---|---|---|
| | Acknowledgments | 10 |
| 1 | How Steve Job's 'Next Big Thing' Changed The Game | 12 |
| 2 | Repositioning | 18 |
| 3 | In Pursuit of Uniqueness | 32 |
| 4 | Making Strategic Adjustment | 44 |
| 5 | When The Industry Is Attacked | 58 |
| 6 | Masters Of The Competition | 70 |
| 7 | Defending An Invasion | 81 |
| 8 | Invading An Industry | 95 |
| 9 | Bonus: The Spirit of Strategy | |

# ACKNOWLEDGMENTS

I acknowledge the faith of our clients in our work globally. Your dream to produce more results keeps me awake at night and focused all day. The result includes this book. Thank you.

I'm hugely indebted to Gbola Onalaja, my Executive Assistant, your commitment and dedication to our work is unparalleled. This book wouldn't have been written without your support. Thank you.

Thank you Juanita Monoto, you're irreplaceable. I can't fully express how deeply grateful I am for your commitment to our work in South Africa and globally. You are unreservedly committed. Thank you.

Finally to my Dad, Reuben Egbulonu who passed away this year. Thank you for sowing the seed of leadership in me. You finished your course and kept the faith. I love you.

# HOW STEVE JOB'S 'NEXT BIG THING' CHANGED THE GAME (A PREFACE)

For every battle of the warrior is with confused noise,
Isaiah 9:5 KJV

On the 19th of August 2020, several news houses reported that Apple just crossed the $2 trillion market capitalization mark, becoming only the second company ever to do so. Apple Inc is definitely a heavyweight in the corporate world today. They occupy a prestigious position many companies only dream of. What began at a garage in California is today the most profitable company in the world with devices, services and ethos interwoven into much of modern daily life. Apple touches the lives of several people around the world in magnificent ways today, giving real meaning to life. That is the true meaning of business, to touch people's lives in an exceptional way while making profit out of it.

Not many however can easily remember that Apple almost signed for bankruptcy just 24 years ago. Things got so bad for Apple that every analyst report indicated that Apple was definitely out of the game. As a matter of fact, Dell CEO, Michael Dell responding to an interview on what he would do if he was the Apple CEO, said he will shut the whole thing down!

But Steve Jobs who just returned to Apple as CEO after he was forced to leave the company in 1986 didn't think so. He thought Apple could not only survive but lead the market. In a 1998 interview after Steve Jobs had saved Apple, he said his next move was to wait for 'the next big thing'.

This next big thing as it turned out was a chaos that overtook the music industry about the same period. His ability to see through the pattern in the chaos gave him the edge to dominate the market. The chaos was his profit.

Market leadership requires an understanding of your Industry and a unique positioning within the industry which gives the business the ability to create and capture value. As long as the industry structure remains unchanged and the business understands and executes their strategy effectively, the business will profit. If the business has a superbly unique business approach, it could lead the market.

But in highly competitive markets as many are today, designing and sustaining a unique position in any industry isn't a simple task. It takes a more-than-casual knowledge of strategy. It takes the executives committed to results rather than excuses, blames and complains. It takes the rare ability to recognize value lapses, competitive loopholes, industry structural imbalances, competitive myopia, strategy gaps, tactical errors and the ability to leverage on them.

This was Steve Job's advantage. He had the ability to see through the chaos in the music industry. He understood that the case in the industry wasn't about piracy as the stakeholders saw it, but about a structural imbalance created by disruption in technology. He knew that managing that imbalance was the key to victory, not court cases. The .mp3 technology had given too much power to music buyers, so reconceiving value delivery in the industry was key to leading the market. He was right, his 'next big thing' was here and he leveraged it so well. His response to this chaos was the iPod and iTunes store and they spelt the beginning of Apple's market leadership.

In 'Art of War for Executives' Donald Krause wrote, 'direct attacks generate emotion. For this reason, develop certain devices which can be used to refocus attention.' Chaos is among the top tools that can get people hyper focused. During chaotic situations a great number of the stakeholders enter into what Wesley Wells called waking trance in 1924 and it refers to the concentration of attention on something. It means being hyper focused on a subject to the exclusion of everything else.

Times of heightened focus are great moments for awakened executives because they know how to leverage them to their competitive advantage.

The key is to do your own thinking independently. You can't even rely on the media and research institutions to understand what is happening because their being compromised might be the real strength of the chaos. In times of chaos keep Newton's words in mind, 'an object either remains at rest or continues to move at a constant velocity, unless acted upon by a force.' So an industry structure will remain at rest or continue to move at a constant speed unless acted upon by a force.' This force will disrupt the state of the industry and give only those who understand it an unfair advantage over the rest of the competition. Your job is to see things beyond how they appear to what they really are.

Through the pages that follow I hope to guide your thoughts on how to respond to chaotic situations strategically to gain competitive advantage.

Dr Brian Reuben
October, 2020.

# CHAPTER ONE

## REPOSITIONING

*The greatest fortunes are made when the cannon balls fall at the harbour, not when the violins play in the ballroom.*
- Nathaniel Rothschild.

"In rapidly evolving systems, **permanent** competitive advantage does not exist; there is only continuous effort to create new sources of temporary but sustainable advantage."

Superior performance is not possible without a clearly designed and executed strategy that creates and sustains an advantage for the firm. This strategy is defined by the uniqueness of the choices the company makes across its value chain, the consistency of those choices and their sustainability.

Determining the right choices to be made usually depends on a clear understanding of the environment where this business will operate in terms of the key players that have the exact influence in the environment and have the power to determine the profitability available in the environment.

Superior performance thus depends on understanding the structure of the business environment or industry and the position of the company in question. This is what gives the company an advantage over competition. This is what separates the company from the pack and makes superior performance possible.

Without a clear advantage, a business has no basis for expecting superior performance, the forces of competition will determine what happens to it and it has no guarantee of even remaining in business. So when the industry is booming it can rise with the tide and fall with it as well.

Strategy is such an important subject in business literature and this is underscored by the results of a search of the academic literature using "strategy" as a keyword: More than four million citations were listed. Amazon lists more than 49,000 books with strategy in the title and a broad Google search shows 800 million hits

Two obvious conclusions can be drawn from this interest: First, Strategy is clearly important; and second, given the disparate approaches, there does not seem to be a consensus about "how" strategy works—in spite of the fact that there is a good consensus on the definition of the term itself. Yet, superior performance is not possible without strategy.

Given the definition that strategy is the positioning of a firm within its competitive environment, it does follow that the company must be repositioned when there is a shift in that competitive environment.

This repositioning first entails the understanding of the industry, what has really changed, what kind of change it is and to what extent the industry changed. The company is then in a better position to make the right choices based on the options the new industry structure now presents.

The outbreak of the corona virus has changed the world and shaken the foundations of many industries. Supply chains have been shaken; policies have been adjusted and just about everything that makes competition work have been challenged. Most of the entire world has slipped into a recession. CNBC reports that the business travel sector will lose $820 billion in revenue on the pandemic. That's a loss of over 50% for a sector worth just a little over a trillion dollars.

How should you respond in a period like this? That's a million dollar question and a situation which definitely requires making hard choices. As a guide I will recommend the following:

- **Review your corporate values and ensure you stay true to it.** In periods of difficulties as it is, you need a compelling reason to stay in business and thrive in the midst of difficulties. Sit with your team and remind yourselves why you got into business in the first instance. Why do you have to do this? Just for the money? That's not good enough! You will need a compelling reason that inspires everyone and that should come from your value. 'We are here because our society needs security. 2000 clients nationwide currently depend on us for this need and through the difficulties we will find a way to stay on and thrive. We believe in **resilience!**'

That's how values can inspire. The more you stay on this the more you see options you never knew were there. You can't fully see all the possible action points, leverages and multiple advantages at your disposal until you strengthen your awareness of your values as an organization. You could reinvent your organization, redesign your offerings and get more value out of your current relationships just by reviewing your corporate values.

- **Understand the exact impact on your industry.** Crises impact different industries in different ways. A negative impact in one industry might mean a positive impact on another and insignificant impact on another. For example, while Unilever Nigeria suffered a revenue loss of 40% for the three month period ending June 2020, MTN Nigeria reported 49% growth in data in the same second quarter of 2020. So a crisis that negatively affects one industry may affect another industry positively.

Cases exist however where an industry may not suffer an immediate impact of a crisis but definitely do later. A case is the real estate industry in Nigeria. In Nigeria, unlike economies like the United States, rental payments for apartments are made on a yearly rather than monthly basis. So at the inception of the coronavirus pandemic the real estate industry seemed unaffected, but experts have insisted that hard times are ahead for the industry as people's rent will eventually run out and they may be unable to renew them. Except things change though the industry is yet to suffer a hit, it eventually will.

Knowing the exact impact on your industry enables you to prepare for yourself and organisation to take the right steps at the right time.

- **Review your critical assets**
  Nucor's key source of competitive advantage is their ability to run their steel mini-mills more cost effectively than any other company. It rewards it's managers very well for achieving this, so much so it became the goal of its plant managers to run the most cost effective plant. One particular year, the manager who ran the most effective plant showed up for his reward and

instead got fired! Why? Well, because top management realized he was undermining plant maintenance thereby stealing from the company's asset base and putting Nucor's long term advantage at risk.

Nucor paid serious attention to it's plant maintenance as that asset held an important advantage to the firm. In your case, it may be your brand that holds the advantage for you. Whatever it is for you, protecting that asset should be top priority for you. The first step is clarity on what your most important assets are and then to measure the impact of the change on those assets.

It could be a brand for some and a distribution network for others. Most times it's more than one thing. Whatever the case may be for your organization, you have to understand it and place appropriate value on it.

Now the thing is value not recognized is value not maximized. It is the responsibility of managers to not only recognize the company's most important assets but to also communicate it to everyone in the organization.

According to Mark Twain, if you got all your eggs in one basket, you should have your eyes on that basket. In a period of crisis, managers must place a premium in protecting the critical assets of the business. Whatever that protection means in your situation, is it's training for your staff, train them. If it's running your plant in the most efficient way, make sure it's done.

- **Review your value chain and reconsider your choices.**
As obvious, every business represents a set of carefully selected activities. This activity based thinking to business demonstrates that everyone in the organization is important in the creation and capturing of value.

As value is created at each activity unit so can it be lost at activity level. Value is lost when the input that is made at a particular activity unit doesn't contribute to the overall value the company takes to the customer. When you invest resources in an input the customer is not willing to pay for that's a loss.

Imagine a budget hotel that provides newspapers in each room. While the guests will love it, they are also prepared to do without it. If that increases the cost of your rooms, guests will quickly choose your competitor that offers a lower rate per room. If you decide to keep your cost at parity with the competition, you lose money. So that's a clear case of a wrong competitive activity.

You see, following industry tradition can be dangerous. You can't afford to make choices you don't have a reason for and you cannot afford to reject an activity for no reason. Every choice you make must be based on clarity and consistent with your strategic approach.

So in times of difficulties it is important you review your value chain to see what needs to be there and what can go. Is there a newer way of processing your product? Is there a new technology? Is the difficulty offering you a chance to integrate vertically? Would you have to outsource something? Do you need to use cheaper packaging? What is your distribution channel like? Is there a need to change that? By reviewing your value chain, you can discover strategic ways to lower your cost or offer more value or both.

- **Remain strategic in the face of difficulties.**
As managers struggle between meeting short term goals in a period of difficulties and keeping pace with long term goals the temptation to abandon their strategic positioning becomes pretty high. I must warn you that it will be a terrible mistake to do that.

Truth is that irrespective of the

difficulties and maybe the narrowness of your approach, there still exists amazing potentials which can be unlocked. But it takes a mind locked on its strategy to see that. Difficult days don't last forever, they come and go. As a manager you cannot afford to throw the baby away just because the bathing water is bad.

You must stay strategic in the face of difficulties. The only exemptions is when upon a review it becomes clear that it is impossible to continue on the same path you have been. Even so, the organization must also be restructured and the value chain reviewed to bring them to the current realities.

If your offers are premium, they should remain so. If you must serve a low cost segment then create a flanker brand because you don't want to be all things to all people and you cannot afford the misalignment in terms of human resources, relationships and other assets that follows changing your strategic position in the middle of the race.

Never let the pursuit of your short term goals override the importance of preserving your strategic position. Understand that while your survival is important, your approach to survival is equally important. Your inability to survive within the constraints of your strategy is a demonstration of strategic incompetence.

Organizations that will thrive in the post coronavirus business world will largely be those guided by ideas such as the ones I have identified here.

No organization can afford to ignore just one of the steps and expect to thrive. In the face of these difficulties, survival depends on responding appropriately to the changes the pandemic presents, thriving will depend on taking advantage of the chaos the pandemic has brought to control the structure of your industry to some extent.

Chaos is an important strategic tool in

changing the competitive structure of an industry because it throws people out of balance and destroys proven competitive advantage of your peers. Covid19 is the biggest chaos in recent history and could leave new industry champions in its wake. Any organization that wants to thrive must prioritize it's strategy review and reassessment.

To understand how to change the competitive structure of your industry email admin@brianreuben.com and request for the training material- CHANGING THE GAME. For free Strategy assessment tools email admin@brianreuben.com with the subject STRATEGY TOOLS.

# CHAPTER TWO

## THE PURSUIT OF UNIQUENESS

*Uniqueness in strategic terms is more than one action. You can have a unique branding and not be unique in the sense of strategy.*
- Dr Brian Reuben

Your competitive advantage depends on your positioning within the industry. This advantage is the only reason why superior performance is possible. Without a competitive advantage you can have only what other players in the industry let you have and you can guess that won't be a great way to compete. This is easy to understand because the opposite of competitive advantage is competitive disadvantage. There is no middle ground.

Managers clearly understand the need for competitive advantage especially after seeing what happened to several during the 2008 economic crisis which shook businesses globally and now the coronavirus pandemic that has hit nations badly. Every manager understands that it takes more than a great corporate goal to win. What many managers don't clearly understand is how to go about establishing this advantage.

As seen in Chapter one, superior performance depends on the management ability to adopt a unique approach to competition. As clear as that is however, it can also be hugely misunderstood.

Uniqueness in strategic terms is more than one action. You can have a unique branding and not be unique in the sense of strategy. You can have a unique product and still lack uniqueness. To understand uniqueness in the sense that I mean, you need to first understand that every business or company is a conglomeration of carefully selected activities which are linked one to another.

The uniqueness of a company in the sense of strategy comes from the summation of the unique activities that make up the entire chain, which Michael Porter called, value chain. Uniqueness comes by not doing activities different from how others do that, but, by linking those activities in a way that is peculiar to your company that it produces a unique fit or configuration that is original to your company.

It is this unique chain of activities that gives a company it's strategic position. Now, triumphing in moments of chaos is a matter of **positioning**. Positioning enables you to control the actions of others to your own advantage.

There is a reason why it's so important to think about these activities in terms of value. This is because being successful is not just about being busy, it is being about the right things. Activities that don't add up to the intended value is meaningless and a waste of effort. This means that companies incur losses or make profit at the activity level. Strategic gains are made at activity level not when the products are sold.

To put this clearer, the gains or losses don't really have much to do with spending less at each activity level. It rather is about spending the right amount. It is about not compromising the strategic promise made to the end user.

That begs the question, what is the right amount? The right amount is the required input arrived at the most efficient way. It's very important to commit only the required effort, knowledge, finances and other assets and no more or less into each value activity.

One way to approach this is to understand that every activity exists in a micro industry with suppliers and buyers as well as substitutes. There is also a micro value chain within each value activity in the company. Lack of clarity about this causes managers to make lousy decisions. Training managers and supervisors to recognize the micro chain, understand the power of their suppliers and buyers within the company as well as their own power is the way to go in the pursuit of strategic uniqueness.

Consider operations in a financial institution, say a bank. Now, the operations department in a bank is a back-end team responsible for executing and settling transactions initiated by the front-end teams. So, the operations value activity depends on the supply from the client-facing roles including marketing and customer care but as well as IT, security, procurement, human resource management and firm infrastructure.

Frictions arise many times when a unit, say, IT fails to meet the expectations of the operations unit for any reason. Yet if strategic uniqueness must be maintained, operations must ensure the adequate investment is made. Imagine when the Human Resource team rejects the proposal of the sales team, or one of its suppliers to sponsor a training for the team because there is a recession and the company cannot afford to train. Sooner or later the team will lose motivation and unable to effectively supply the finance unit which depends on them. The end result is failure. Yet this type of scenario plays out each day.

Solving this problem requires that each value activity unit must think in terms of the activities that depend on them just like the marketing value activity must think in terms of the client. They must realize that their real value is their ability to satisfy those they serve in the most efficient way. It's therefore more appropriate for the inbound logistics value activity unit to focus on the operations and other units that buy from them with the company than the final clients.

On the other side, each value activity unit must design a competitive strategy since resources are limited. If every activity unit has a competitive advantage, it will eventually get to the shareholders and investors. Marketing needs a competitive advantage to get the required investment and support from their suppliers including HR and IT. It's not going to happen just because they are part of the organization. Same goes to other activity units in the organization including the C-Suite if they intend to have the required efforts and investment from the shareholders.

**The Unique Value Proposition**
This is the promise the company makes to it's intending clients. This promise must be distinct and compelling enough to get the required attention. Several organizations compete for the attention of the same group of people, out-competing others and securing the results you intend will require that your promise is distinct and superior from all the other ones. It's to this proposition that you design a unique value chain which aligns with it.

People only buy your offer when the perceived value of your product or service exceeds what they have to invest to have it. When they think the value of your offer is less or equal to what it will cost them, they will walk away. So people walk away not because they don't need what you offer, but more because they don't think they are gaining more than they have to pay.

Offering people a compelling value then must begin with your understanding of what their total cost looks like.

### How Value Is Delivered

| Acquisition Costs + | Possession Cost + | Usage Cost = |
|---|---|---|
| **TOTAL CUSTOMER COST** | | |
| 1. Price | 1. Interest cost | 1. Field defects |
| 2. Paperwork | 2. Storage cost | 2. Training costs |
| 3. Shopping time | 3. Quality control | 3. User labour cost |
| 4. Expediting cost | 4. Taxes and insurance | 4. Product longievity |
| 5. Mistake in order cost | 5. Shrinkage and obsolescence | 5. Replacement cost |
| 6. Pre-purchase product evaluation costs | 6. General internal handling cost | 6. Disposal costs |

When you understand the total cost, your job is to use that as a leverage to show the intending clients that the cost of *not* investing in your offer far exceeds the pain and cost of investing and that investing in your offer rather removes their cost and pain than increases it.

This was how Becton Dickinson which we discussed in chapter one managed to sell their Hypodermic needle at 65% higher than the market rate and yet controlled 60% of the market share.

The secret was in the company effectively framing a compelling value proposition and aligning it to a unique value chain. When a Becton Dickinson salesman meets with the purchasing manager at the hospital, he proposes he can save the company hundreds of thousands of dollars if only they let them explain. The explanation that follows shows how the hospital spends xyz dollars on disposal cost by employing its own staff. Now Becton Dickinson sales man promises to make all of that cost go away because Becton Dickinson will take care of disposal and let the hospital either reassign its disposal staff with all the risk involved in keeping them or dismiss them if they prefer. Becton Dickinson will take up the disposal leveraging their knowledge and experience in handling such operations if only the hospital will buy their needles at their stated cost.

A hesitation from the hospital purchasing manager will be met by the Becton Dickinson sales man promises to put down half the fees of a CPA to carry out an activity based costing to show the hospital how much they are really spending on disposal. This way, he reveals an advantage even greater than the cost of the needles. They promised the hospital product liability insurance which holds the risk of the hospital being shut down if taken lightly if they buy their needles. How compelling that can be!

**Strategic positioning is a question of uniqueness.**

But, a unique value proposition isn't just from the company to the clients. Just as the company must hold up a unique value proposition to its clients so must the various value activity units within the organization. IT must show a compelling reason if they expect it's demand on the scarce dollar to be approved by accounts. It has to go beyond a right to compelling reason. This is the right picture in the pursuit of uniqueness. When every unit is cultured to make a compelling case otherwise subject it's supply to what's available, losses are eliminated and gains appreciate at the value activities. This gives a company a fit no competitor can successfully copy.

While I was leading a training at an oil and gas company and told the story of Becton Dikenson, a commercial manager quickly asked why their competitors didn't quickly copy this approach. The answer is that the ability to deliver on that promise resides in the value chain and includes even the organizational culture. Effective strategy is hardly the result of one choice, it's always about a systematic sophistication in a business approach.

Copying just that one unique promise cannot work. The only way that can work is if you imported the whole Becton Dikenson including their values into your company. That's nearly impossible and that's what it means to have a sustainable business approach.

# CHAPTER THREE

## MAKING STRATEGIC ADJUSTMENTS

*When the light chariots come out first and take up a position on the wings, it is a sign that the enemy is forming for battle.*
- Sun Tzu

Dominating an industry is a matter of positioning. Your position gives you a competitive advantage relative to your peers.

Without a strategic position it is impossible to sustain a superior performance. Like we see in chapter two, positioning is distinguishing a company in its environment. To position a company strategically, you must understand the competitive power play in that industry that determines what's possible and how things are done. This is what Michael Porter calls **forces of competition.**

According to Porter, there are five forces that shape competition. This runs contrary to what some managers are conscious of. It is very easy to think about competition in terms of your peers selling the same solution as you do to the same market. These are the ones you describe as your rivals.

But these may be the least of your problems when you talk about competition. Porter identified four other 'forces' capable of taking away the revenue and profitability available to an organization. These are your suppliers and buyers, then solutions that substitute yours and an unseen 'force' which Porter called, 'barriers to entry into the industry.'

These put together shape the competition within an industry and how business is done. In some industries like the airline, the barrier to entry is high because of huge capital investments required to run an airline but there are many substitutes. The buyers are very price sensitive and the only real attraction to an airline could just be the price of the tickets. Passengers are willing to move to another airline for just a minor price difference. And especially for domestic flights. Someone can get on the train or even drive a car and sacrifice time.

Then, they have to still deal with suppliers who are very powerful and can thus bargain profit away. Aeroplane manufacturers are powerful and have lots of bargaining advantages over the airline operators. At the snap of your fingers you can count how many airlines that have failed and the number struggling.

This makes the airline industry look unattractive. Infact, the billionaire British businessman, Richard Branson said the only way to end up as a millionaire in the airline industry is to begin as a billionaire.

Does it mean it's impossible to profit in the industry? Absolutely not! An airline like the South West Airlines by understanding their industry structure and managing the forces of the industry has maintained a leadership position in the industry. That's the essence of Strategy! The strategic executive understands where the money is in the industry and designs a position that enables him to get the money.

But, you see the structure of this industry makes competition intense but not just with other airline operators but with suppliers, substitutes and the buyers. To profit in this industry then, you must consider and carefully design an approach that can give you some form of advantage over the forces of competition in the industry.

In the case of an industry like healthcare where the patients have less bargaining power. When someone is sick the main concern is recovery. You don't even want a cheaper drug, you want what works. So buyers in this industry have less advantage than suppliers and the healthcare providers do. So competition is not just with those offering the same value as you but with other stakeholders.

Considering all of these 'forces', the company must now design an approach to competition that puts them in a position of advantage. And this position remains useful only as the structure of the competition remains the same. When the competitive landscape shifts, the organization must be repositioned. That's just common sense.

**Shifting Landscapes**

*In evolutionary systems, sustainable competitive advantage does not exist; there is only a never ending race to create new sources of temporary advantage.* - **Eric D. Beinhocker**

There has been a never ending debate whether or not it's possible to have a sustainable competitive advantage given our rapidly changing business environment.

Well, the first thing is to understand that there is no such thing as a permanent competitive advantage. Every advantage is industry specific and is relevant as long as the structure of the industry remains unchanged.

Years back, when the environment was more predictable and stable, organizations can be certain that their strategy and the plan based on it will carry them through some five years or three years. In the past commercial patterns were predictable, so organisations were designed for efficiency and effectiveness. Today commercial patterns are quite unpredictable, rather than just efficiency, organisations must be designed for agility, adaptability and speed so that they can thrive in today's highly disruptive environment. Being effective today will first of all require an organisation structured for speed, agility and adaptability.

So, can a competitive advantage be sustainable? It's useless if it can't be. While changes happen rapidly, organizations must be structured to drive strategic adjustments as often as necessary. That way the strategic advantage becomes sustainable because reviews are scenario driven rather time-driven. Just as you can sustain the service of a car so long as you carry out the necessary periodic maintenance so can a competitive advantage be sustained through scenario based approach.

According to Jack Welch, If the rate of change on the outside exceeds the rate of change on the inside, the end is near. Strategic effectiveness requires an intelligent structure able to understand the environment and how it is changing as well as the ability to respond strategically.

In designing a strategic position, a clear understanding of the industry structure is key and attention is to be given to the most significant force(s).

But the forces of competition might shift and when that happens your strategic position comes under an attack. It may look insignificant initially, yet ignoring that might be the beginning of a serious problem.

That is the story behind the massive success of Apple's iPod which recorded more than five million songs downloads from the iTunes store within the first two months.

The revolution began with the development of the .mp3 format in the mid-1990s which provided a means to store audio in a compressed format that was far smaller than uncompressed audio. With the relatively small hard drives of the time, this enabled people to store their music collection on their personal computers, and create their own compact discs of mixed compilations.

The natural progression from the .mp3 was the development of Internet-based file sharing platforms. Beginning with Napster, launched in 1999, many large-scale file sharing applications proliferated, all designed to help the illegal sharing of .mp3 files.

Many artists and record labels filed lawsuits against the offending companies, and also against people exploiting the platforms. Although some progress was made in curbing the use of these sites, there were still millions of Americans who downloaded pirated music.

One of the first companies to try to legitimise downloading of single tracks was Apple, which opened its iTunes music store in 2002 to complement its iPod device. This way redefined the competitive landscape and created a competitive advantage for themselves. But they didn't stop there because they understood that whatever advantage they have could only be for a moment. So again they came with their iPhone and that way began a new world of telecommunication. Again that gave them a competitive advantage.

While the players in the music industry were running to preserve the industry structure, Apple understood that what mattered was positioning their company to profit from a changed competitive landscape.

That sounds like how Blockbuster responded when Netflix took off. Rather than adjust to change in the industry landscape, Blockbuster chose to deny the power of the change. According to reports, early public statements by Blockbuster dismissed the notion that its customers would benefit from an online rental business. In May

2002, a spokesperson addressed the online rental market: "Obviously, we pay attention to any way people are getting home entertainment. We always look at all those things. We have not seen a business model that's financially viable long-term in this arena. Online rental services are 'serving a niche market.'"

Three months later, clarifying that Blockbuster did not intend to launch an online business to compete with Netflix, a spokesperson announced, "We don't believe there is enough of a demand for mail order—it's not a sustainable business model." Furthermore, the 2002 annual report made only a cursory mention of the threat posed by online rental websites, with no mention at all in the "Risks" according to Pete Barlas. Today Netflix market capitalisation is in excess of $100 billion, Blockbuster is bankrupt!

But that's not something new. Henry Ford years ago presumed that consumers would continue to want black autos in the face of evidence that they were becoming more interested in color. IBM doggedly pursued PC hardware while Intel usurped the microprocessor market and Microsoft dominated the software for PC operating systems. Jim Balsillie, *Research in Motion* ex executive who was the maker of the BlackBerry suggested that the iPhone wouldn't make it very far. There are now over 700 million iPhone users in the world currently according to an estimate from BMO Capital Markets analyst Tim Long. At its peak in September 2013, there were 85 million BlackBerry subscribers worldwide. However, BlackBerry has since lost its dominant position in the market; the same numbers had fallen to 23 million in March 2016.

Why do executives deny the obvious? Well, Because it is often easier, "safer," and more profitable in the short run, and more comfortable than confronting a problem, a poor decision made by a superior executive, a difficult personnel decision, or a failing strategy. Of course denial can sometimes lead to remarkable achievements against all odds, particularly for entrepreneurs nurturing start-ups but it can be destructive and very expensive in other cases.

I think denial is endemic to management. But why does it happen in the first instance? First it is normal for human beings to deny what they are afraid of or don't understand. It is much associated with the survival instinct in human beings. According to Neuroscience, once we solve a particular problem in a particular way several times, the brain stops looking for new ways of solving the problem. The same applies to organisations. But then denial is just one part of the problem; not understanding your capabilities and resources is even a bigger issue.

What does this mean to an organization in working out its strategy? What should you do when a shift takes place in your industry? History is a great teacher and we can choose to be its student. Whatever that was written aforetime was written for our learning, that we through the comfort and insights they provide can make premium decisions.

The lessons from all the cases highlighted above can be summarized as follows:

1. Denying shifts in the competitive landscape is an endemic problem that must be dealt with right now,
2. Facts have to be confronted and analysed not avoided,

3. An organisational environment where truth can be spoken to the leaders can be a strategic asset,
4. Leadership behaviors such as listening are essential,
5. Behaviors designed to optimize the short-term may themselves be symptoms of denial,
6. Words matter; when words are used to hide facts, denial may be near,
7. While every move by the competition may not be a threat, each one must be considered with an open mind to see chances of threat short term and long term and
8. It is better to be unconventional and right than it is to be conventional and possibly wrong, as in the old saying among information technology managers that "nobody ever got fired for buying IBM."

# CHAPTER FOUR

## WHEN THE INDUSTRY IS ATTACKED

*For the past 33 years, I have looked in the mirror every morning and asked myself: 'If today were the last day of my life, would I want to do what I am about to do today?' And whenever the answer has been 'No' for too many days in a row, I know I need to change something.*
   - Steve Jobs

Netflix's attack on the film rental industry was phenomenal. They figured out a way to compete on a different dimension from the major players like Blockbuster and Video City. The structure of the industry included Realtors who supplied rental shops and video studios who supplied video tapes.

Suppliers possessed huge power because location was key and the movies stocked at each store determined movie rental success. Stores were reluctant to stock larger numbers of lesser-known and independent films since the demand for such titles was inconsistent. Rental companies usually stock a narrow selection of mostly familiar movies. The cost of stocking these new movies were however high giving the rental companies less bargaining power with the studios.

Profitability required getting the highest returns on these popular movies. In the case of Blockbuster, movies not returned to the same locations where they were rented by the end of the specified rental period were subject to extended viewing fees. In 2004, 10 percent of Blockbuster revenues came from late fees representing $600 million. This arrangement didn't give clients much choice but remained a source of pain for them.

As the world evolved and new technology arrived, Netflix CEO, Reed Hastings figured out movie DVDs can be rented through an online subscription-based model. This model has been inspired by his pain of paying $40 extended viewing fee of an overdue rented copy of a movie he had rented. Hastings model was an online movie rental service company delivering through the U.S Postal Service. Thereby doing away with brick and mortar stores and saving cost. They eventually also figure out how to effectively rent lesser known movies, which of course cost less to their clients. This way Hastings and his new company Netflix were able to bypass the traditional suppliers of the movie rental industry and thus restructure the industry!

As this attack on the industry took off, Blockbuster simply dismissed it's success and declared that Netflix's model was not sustainable. Well, today Blockbuster is bankrupt! Every new business model is an attack on the industry. When it succeeds, it changes the competitive dynamics. An industry is attacked when a new company enters the industry with a new value chain or solution that threatens the power of any of the forces of competition in that industry. When this happens every competitor must reposition themselves or strengthen their position depending on the nature of the attack.

## Understanding How To Attack An Industry

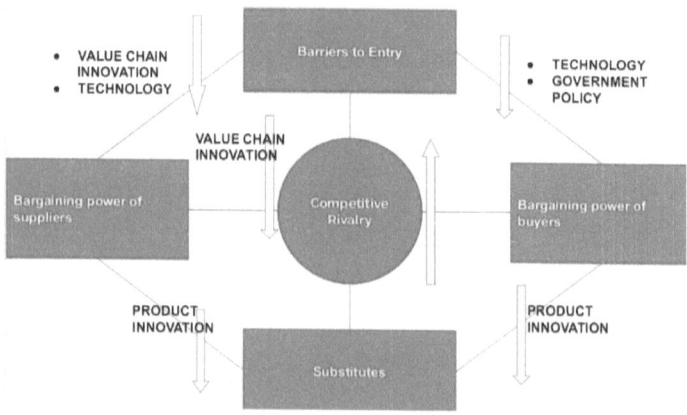

According to Peter Drucker, there are only two duties of the Enterprise, innovation and marketing. These two are so important to the success of the Enterprise that any business will at best merely survive without them. Throughout history, organizations that remain are only those that understood innovation and have it as a corporate culture.

Innovation is translated from the Latin word *innovare* which means to reform or to change. It means to do something differently. So this is not dealing with new, it's about reforming or doing differently.

It is through innovation that the forces of competition can be challenged. By innovating any aspect of the industry structure, it either loses or gains strength and thus the competitive landscape shifts.

As pictured above, technology can shift any of the five 'forces'. Through technology the barrier to entry can be lowered or increased. It was technology that enabled companies like Multichoice in South Africa to lower the cost of satellite TV services given millions access to the service.

Digital terrestrial television is a technology for terrestrial television in which land-based (terrestrial) television stations broadcast television content by radio waves to televisions in consumers' residences in a digital format lowering the operation cost significantly. A new market was thus born, the power of the suppliers broken and substitute created. That's an attack on the industry.

It was through technology that Apple restructured the music industry and brought in new possibilities with losers and gainers. Technology can completely eliminate or at least reduce the strength of a competitive 'force'. With Apple's attack, the entry barrier was adjusted, the product was redefined, giving more gains to the buyer but reducing their bargaining power and the power of the suppliers was weakened. That's what technology can do.

In the case of Kodak, their power in the picture industry was lost when they took technology changes for granted. Technology brought in the power to redefine the industry and what service they provided but Kodak looked the other way.

At best Kodak can be described as the architect of its own failure. A Kodak engineer, Steve Stevenson had invented a digital camera(though it was as big as a toaster and took 20 seconds to take a picture) and presented it to his company in 1975. Rather than perfect on that innovation, the management reacted negatively to it and instructed him not to tell anyone about the concept. They rather focused on photographic film where they had a competitive advantage. Kodak failed to reimagine their business and that landed them into bankruptcy.

Innovating the business model is another approach to industry attack. According to George Box, 'all models are wrong; the practical question is how wrong do they have to be to not be useful. What this means is that no business model is free from errors. It is human beings that at one point in time in the pursuit of their objectives and based on their perspective created the model and such model is limited by their perspectives, knowledge, experience and interest. There is therefore a certain level of results that is possible through a particular business model. By approaching the same business through another model, the results can differ significantly.

According to an IBM Global CEO Study in 2006 which interviewed 765 corporate and public sector leaders from around the world on the subject of innovation, competitive pressures have pushed business model innovation much higher than expected on CEOs' priority lists. The study revealed that profits outperformers focused on business model innovation rather than product or process innovation.

What Apple did through technology wasn't just a product or process innovation, it was a business model innovation. **Business model innovation was behind Google's huge success.** October 23, 2000, the birth of the first ever self-serve online advertising platform – Google AdWords. By the end of their first year, Google ads had returned over $70 million. Google made $24.1 billion revenue for Q3 2018 from advertising.

How was this possible? Google attacked the advertising industry with a business model innovation. Google gave the advertisers more options by giving them the chance to set up their advert themselves. A sure smart move that also lowered Google operation cost as they introduce that do-it-yourself model. While traditional advert companies offered **Pay per placement, rigid, company controlled option with no feedback**, Google offered a pay per click or impression and flexible, self service with feedback mechanism. That changed the industry forever.

IKEA's approach was however very different. The focus was different. The focus was value chain innovation. IKEA made a very clear choice of where they want to play in the furniture industry. Their focus was on young, first time, or price-sensitive buyers with design sophistication who want stylish, space efficient and compatible furniture lines and accessories at very low price points.

To achieve this they have to be able to innovate the traditional furniture value chain. If they followed the traditional furniture value chain, they can't deliver on their promise. They needed a different set of activities to deliver value. The result of this decision to innovate the value chain is now a US$45.4 billion multinational company serving a market that hitherto didn't exist.

Value chain innovation begins by reimagining the service. As you reimagine the service, you can see new ways to offer it and new markets to serve. Many times, it becomes impossible to serve this new market at a profit without altering how value is created in the industry.

A useful approach many times, is to identify all the separate activities within the traditional value chain and challenge them. Why should they be there? Are there other ways of performing them? Are they necessary at all? Can they be performed at a lower cost? Such eye opening questions can help produce a completely new set of activities for creating and capturing value in the industry.

Industry changes do not happen on their own, they result from the thoughts and efforts of strategists deliberately shifting industry structure in their advantage. This understanding helps the executive identify and properly respond to the activities of industry players irrespective of how subtle they look.

When in the 1980s Coca-Cola began buying bottling companies, that was a clear attack on the industry intended to raise barriers to entry since the Bottlers buy concentrates from the carbonated soft drink makers and bottled them for distribution. By buying and controlling the bottling segment of the industry, intending entrants can be discouraged from getting into the industry.

That's similar to Nokia's intense investment in knowledge assets in the years of their glory before the industry was completely restructured. Nokia had a substantial patent portfolio with over 1600 new fillings in 2005 making it almost impossible for any mobile phone to be made without using several of Nokia's patents. That was a clear effort and success at controlling the industry supply and except for the complete restructuring of the industry Nokia would not have fallen.

# CHAPTER FIVE

## MASTERS OF THE COMPETITION

*Effective strategy is formless and invisible, rivals don't know what to defend against.*

It was around 1997 and 1998 that digital music became a big thing and had a major influence, with mp3 files illegally ripped and exchanged from CDs among college students especially. The whole music industry in the United States got into panic about what was really going on. It was a big problem for the college students to stop buying the CDs and rather have music on their computers. Legal battles against such companies as Napster which actually enabled people to download music files from the internet by the music companies followed.

After about 18 months, they got ruling in their favor and got Napster to shut down. In the real sense however, the victory was an empty one as the music industry lost 90% of its revenue. How does an industry continue to exist after losing 90% of its revenue? With only 10% revenue left competition will become intense, many will shut down and jobs will be lost. The industry needed a saviour.

Apple had only recently survived bankruptcy courtesy of Steve Jobs business ingenuity. Asked in 1998, by Richard Rummelt, what he was going to do next, in order to move Apple beyond its fragile niche position, Jobs responded that he will wait for the next big thing. As the crisis in the music industry was on, Mr Jobs didn't see a piracy problem as the music companies did, he rather saw this as an impact of digital technology on the industry. His thought was, how should the music industry operate in a digital world?

That question was the inspiration behind the iPod and eventually iTunes. His intervention, it was that saved the music industry. **Apple in this case is what I describe as an industry keeper.** Imagine what it meant for an industry to lose 90 percent of its revenue! Now remember that an industry is beyond the primary rivals. An industry includes the suppliers of labor and materials. Beyond that an industry growth or decline impacts end users as well as other businesses that depend on the industry to function. So you understand what it means that 90 percent of the revenue in the industry slipped out of their hands. That's very serious.

Many times it's easy to think that it is the sole responsibility of the government to preserve competition and keep an industry. And it can be difficult not to think that way considering man's inborn desire which is actually motivated by fear to control others. This is the reason laws like the *antitrust* in the United States exist. Other countries have similar laws too. In India it's called *Monopolies and Restrictive Trade Practices Act, Antimonopoly Law in* Japan etc.

Through interventions like this, the government indeed keeps the competition for the good of all. But tremendous gains truly come when managers understand how the disposition to keep the competition has a tremendous advantage. A commitment to sustainable competition demands taking responsibility for the preservation of the industry by every stakeholder in the industry.

This was a lesson Microsoft was forced to learn when the Department of Justice and Attorney Generals of 20 different states brought antitrust charges against Microsoft in 1998. to determine whether the company's bundling of additional programs into its operating system constituted monopolistic actions. The suit resulted from the browser wars that led to the collapse of Microsoft's top competitor, Netscape, which occurred when Microsoft began giving away its browser software for free.

After a tough legal battle, the government won the case. There is now no browser monopoly, and the world has come to rely on the many apps, firms and ideas that were born after Microsoft's control was broken.

Can you imagine a world where Microsoft had been allowed to monopolize the browser business. Holding power over the operating system, major applications and the browser, Microsoft would have controlled the future of the web. Google, the tiny start-up, would have faced an unfair fight against Bing.

When Steve Jobs returned to Apple in 1997, the company was in serious distress. In fact, at this time Apple's financial situation was so dire that Dell CEO and founder Michael Dell, once said that if he were Apple CEO, he'd "shut it down and give the money back to the shareholders."

During the final quarter of 1996, Apple's sales plummeted by 30 percent. Microsoft was the dominant computer company in the market. At this time every industry report about

Apple was negative, share prices were falling sharply and everyone was sure bankruptcy was imminent.

Jobs' approach upon return was not to create new products. Talking to investors wasn't a great idea, the banks won't listen either. It was a dead end. Yet Jobs was determined to turn the company around.

His response was to take an assessment of Apple's assets in the face of this crisis. One of such assets was Microsoft's on-going antitrust case against the government. If Bill Gates and Microsoft wanted anything, it was to prove their cases beyond all reasonable doubts that it wasn't playing dirty. Steve Jobs offered Bill Gates and Microsoft the chance to prove this by saving Apple. The result was a $150 million investment in Apple stock by Mr Gates and Apple was saved.

This is the right attitude in competition. It is an approach that enables everyone to win. The truth about competitive effectiveness is that market leadership comes with a responsibility to protect the industry not just for your own good but for the good of others too. The big picture is that competition is about people, not stock price and profitability. This value is very vital for corporate creativity and innovation.

Keeping the competition means giving others the chance to win. It is a commitment to the success of the industry not just a myopic company interest. The thing is, laws like the antitrust and the Glass Stegal would have been unnecessary if organizations are bold enough to commit to keeping the industry. It is the responsibility of the competitive-strong to keep the weak and allow their strength to grow.

Competition is healthy and sustainable when everyone is committed to improving lives for the end users of the product or service and not necessarily making more profit than rivals. The idea is to measure productivity by the gap between the organisation's capacity and their results rather than financial performance or the stock market. This is a much higher perspective than a narrow focus on financial performance because done right it also guarantees healthy financial performance.

Companies that act otherwise do so as a result of competitive myopia, which is the inability to see the competition beyond the rivalry between your peers in the industry. This is the reason for protecting narrow interest and seeking for ways to eliminate others. The thinking here is that for your company to succeed your peers have to lose. That's a very lousy way of thinking about competition.

When Apple was in distress Microsoft did the right thing. The idea wasn't to finally take the oxygen support off Apple so Microsoft will be the biggest competitor. Though I don't know how Microsoft would have responded to the Apple situation if there weren't monopolistic concerns about them. But, by Microsoft investing $150 million for 150,000 shares of preferred stock, convertible to common shares of Apple stock at a price of $8.25, redeemable after a three year period, Microsoft demonstrated leadership. Microsoft will later convert all of its shares into common stock, netting the company approximately 18.1 million shares and selling everything by 2003.

The world is better because Apple remained in business. That was made possible by the commitment of Microsoft. A commitment which rather than diminish their advantage helped increase their reputation value.

Apple will turn around to save the music industry in 2011 through the invention of the iPod. The music industry worth $60 billion in 1996 has lost roughly $15 billion in 1998 as a result of the devastating consequences of free music download. By 2008, the value of the industry was $4.2 billion. But by 2012 after the invention of the iPod in. 2014 revenue climbed to $16.5 billion! The industry was saved. The case may have been different had Microsoft not saved Apple.

The keeping of the competition is never an idea pursued as a charity stunt, rather it is a strategic tool which can give any company a clear competitive advantage. So responding to industry threats requires careful analysis of the strategic implementations and cost. The important thing is to be driven by the desire to see everyone win. Because you see, competition should bring out the best out of businesses and not otherwise. Knowing that others are improving should inspire you to innovate too which makes the world better. Protecting the industry or a peer in the industry not only establishes your position as an industry leader, it can endear you to customers and regulators can strengthen your position.

# CHAPTER SIX

# DEFENDING AN INDUSTRY INVASION

**As in the military, an industry can be invaded.** This was what we established in the previous chapter. Lousy industries will hardly be the choice of an invasion. But when industry profitability is high, the barrier to entry is high with less substitutes, chances of invasion will be high. When the power the suppliers have is however low and bargaining power of buyers is low, industry attack becomes even more compelling.

Many times at the center of the decision to invade an industry is the same reason why nations invade other territories- power and control. For businesses, they invade other markets to increase market size, especially as industry rivalry intensifies. Industry invasion increases the revenue the invaders will have access to. But invasions motivated by the sole desire for increased profitability is selfish and leaves destruction and many casualties in its wake.

Every change in an industry is not necessarily an invasion. An invasion is the concealed act of the competent executive. He causes the competition to respond to his carefully designed circumstances that moves everyone out of balance. When everyone is out of balance, he takes control because he is the only one ready. He strikes with deadly accuracy because of positioning and timing. Like a diving falcon he cannot miss his target.

Competition is a more serious issue than most executives understand. No statement or action of the strategically competent executive is unconnected with his desire to lead the industry. Even seeming failures and mistakes are many times not what they seem.

Understanding industry invasion is important. Sometimes that's the only way to break the iron rod of monopolists with monopolistic powers over an industry. There are companies, sometimes state-owned which profit, not by providing valuable services but because they have exclusive authority from the government. Sometimes, it's a cartel which holds the world to ransom, with absolute control over an industry.

Sometimes when a company has a position of advantage it can become reluctant or too slow to change even when such change can enable it to give more value. Making changes is difficult and if possible many companies can completely avoid it. Most times it's only organizations with weak competitive advantage or no advantage at all that take change seriously but that shouldn't be so. A competitively competent organization understands that except they make their advantage obsolete by out innovating the industry, an impending change would outdo them.

Change in every industry or sector is only a matter of time, you either be the innovator with the change, or when it eventually happens, it sweeps you off your feet.

Think about Eastman Kodak. What happened to Eastman Kodak remains a sad story of the corporate collapse of an industry giant. Precisely on the 19th of January, 2013, Kodak filed for Chapter 11 Bankruptcy protection. This was not only an economic tragedy for a corporate giant, but devastating for New York which had over 60, 000 of its citizens under the employ of Kodak. At its height, Kodak's market share of the photographic film market was over 80% in the U.S. and about 50% globally. Yet that failure was not supposed to happen. It was much like the story of the telecom giant, *Research in Motion* which at its best boasted of over 65 million subscribers but saw that number drop by over 60% within three years. These failures were not necessary, they were avoidable. But they happened for one simple reason, fighting change as a defense to a position of advantage.

At best Kodak can be described as the architect of its own failure. A Kodak engineer, Steve Season had invented a digital camera(though it was as big as a toaster and took 20 seconds to take a picture) and presented it to his company in 1975. Rather than perfect on that innovation, the management reacted negatively to it and instructed him not to tell anyone about the concept. They rather focused on photographic film where they had the competitive advantage.

Why would Kodak do this? Eastman Kodak was a giant in the photography market in the United States, making money from everything connected with the process of photography.

Back then Kodak had a virtual monopoly on the photography market, and according to The Economist, by 1976 the company accounted for 85 percent of camera sales in the United States. When one considers these numbers, it is no wonder that Eastman Kodak's executives were threatened by Sasson's camera, which didn't use film.

Though they permitted him to continue working on the digital camera and in 1978 the first digital camera was patented, they reportedly made Sasson's bosses strictly forbade him to talk publicly about his invention or show the prototype he created to people outside Kodak.

Kodak eventually made billions of dollars from this patent until 2007 when it expired. Unwilling to invest and compete in digital technology, Kodak signed for bankruptcy protection in 2012. Kodak failed to lead an industry revolution set in motion by its own engineer. Others leveraged the technology Kodak invented to invade the industry and ousted Kodak!

Kodak's response was wrong! And now it's clear, because the result is evident. When all considerations indicate that an invasion is imminent, it will amount to competitive irresponsibility to think you can hide behind a large reputation or goodwill.

When an important issue or critical market is threatened, you are already in a weak position. Except you respond in the most competitively intelligent way, you may be heading to the door.

In 2010 as competitive pressure from Android and iPhone built against Nokia, it was clear Nokia had to make an important decision regarding its operating system. Pressure has been building against what once was once the giant of the phone industry since 2008 so much so Nokia's new CEO Stephen Elop compared the Nokia situation to that of a man on a 'Burning Platform'.

In a memo he shared with his staff, Elop urged the company to embrace its own 'radical change in behavior' before it was too late. He wrote, 'I have learnt that we are standing on a burning platform. And, we have multiple points of scorching heat that are fueling a blazing fire around us [...]. Why did we fall behind when the world around us evolved? [...] Some of it has been due to our attitude inside Nokia.'

Nokia was already in a weak position. At this time, it was competitively irresponsible to hide behind a big name. Nokia decided to replace its symbian operating system with Microsoft Windows Phone 7 software. Nokia also approached Google to discuss using Android, but Elop later abandoned that plan explaining that Nokia needed to fight. He said, Nokia shouldn't be just another company distributing Android. Choosing Android may have saved Nokia because it's reputation may have been an advantage among the phones running Android.

Nokia abandoned Android choosing rather to go for Windows. The 14% fall of Nokia's share on the day of the Windows announcement showed much faith investors had with Nokia's decision. Nothing remained the same for Nokia as it struggled through 2012 and 2013. By September 2013 Nokia eventually sold it's Devices and Services business to Microsoft . Upon the announcement of this deal Nokia's share price increased by 40% showing investors lost faith in Nokia's management rather than the products.

Why does this happen? It's because most executives don't understand the difference between changes in the industry and industry invasion. As a result they respond with the wrong strategy tools. In the face of an industry invasion some companies will resort to cutting cost. Others begin overhead cost reduction.

Overhead cost reduction, downsizing, rightsizing, corporate restructuring and others simply get the company to focus inside rather than outside where the real issues are thereby making them competitively blind.

The case with IBM was different. With a 70% control of the information technology industry profits, the company was a clear industry leader. By 1990, they were the second most profitable company in the world. Between 1991 to 1993 however, the company lost nearly $16 billion.

How did this happen? First, computing moved away from the mainframe architecture (responsible for huge portions of IBM's revenue and profits) to the client/server model. Second, computers became commodity hardware with interoperable parts running interoperable technologies. This interoperability pushed prices lower, but IBM's managers could not break from their high-margin mainframe sales to compete in other areas. So, again we meet an industry under attack and a company making wrong decisions.

The situation was turned around as a result of CEO Lou Gerstner's strategic insight. Lou was formerly of RJR Nabisco, American Express, and McKinsey and was brought in to save the company after the CEO, John Akers and his executive team's recovery plan failed to deliver intended results.

The first thing the new CEO did was to reconnect IBM with who they really are. D. Quinn Mills revealed in a MIT Sloan Management Review article that Lou Gerstner did not take IBM on a new course as much as he returned it to its roots. IBM had strayed from their strategy of supplying one-stop shopping for information services to large firms and as such confused and angered its customers.

Next was a recognition of the capabilities at this time. They accepted the truth about themselves and began to compete only where they had the ability to.

**Lou Gerstner understood that survival depends on careful defense and you can't defend a lost ground. You can either plan an offensive to recover the ground or enlist a powerful general to help you.** The information technology industry moved on and IBM stayed behind. Its core business in mainframes has died as a serious computing arena, and IBM is organizationally unsuited to compete in the PC market.

Over in China, a little known company outside China was gearing up to become a global player in the global PC market. *Legend* has maintained market leadership in China for 5 consecutive years but had new challenges dominating this local market with China's entry into the World Trade Organisation. This is because Legend can no longer count on local player advantages as the government imposed quotas and tariffs on imports, or restrictions on foreign companies' ownership rights, investment and access to distribution channels. Put succinctly, the entry barrier has lowered. Legend had to put in the work on its part because it had the intention on its part to become a *Fortune 500* company, therefore changed its name to Lenovo because it noticed there were already other businesses using the name *Legend* outside China.

IBM has a huge reputation, Legend had the resources and the will power to contend for and hopefully recover IBM's lost ground. IBM was ready to sell its Personal Systems Division for $1.75 billion, paying $650 million in cash and upto $600 million in common stock and assuming $500 million IBM liabilities. For IBM, this deal was an opportunity to shed off an area where it was competitively weak and focus on areas of its competitive strength. This was the decision that saved IBM! They did the right thing and they did it fast enough!

When an industry is invaded, you must reposition yourself or take a bow.

Facebook's response to industry invasion is spectacularly different. Their approach is acquisition of potential threats to their dominance. Facebook has acquired 82 other companies, including WhatsApp. The WhatsApp acquisition closed at a steep $16 billion; more than $40 per user of the platform according to Wikipedia.

Facebook has been accused of anticompetitive conduct, including buying up competing tech firms and copying features from rival apps. The Facebook approach can weaken competition and limit the choice of buyers. It was such circumstances for which Microsoft was sued by the Department of Justice and a coalition of 20 state attorneys general in 1998.

In the next chapter we will discuss how to invade an industry and when it's necessary.

# CHAPTER SEVEN

## INVADING AN INDUSTRY

*...the world, with all its times of trouble, still moves ahead. No man can play a big part in the world who does not believe in the future of the world...*
- Bruce Barton.

The world has changed in tremendous ways because of technology. Every technological breakthrough is a celebration of man's ability to challenge his limitations and expand his possibilities. Technology breakthroughs make industry expansion possible, increase productivity, increase efficiency and increase products' value. As the world evolves, as new ways of solving problems are discovered, as new tools for work emerge freedom can be further extended to more and more people.

In the year 2000, the glory days of film photography, Kodak announced that consumers around the world had taken 80 billion photos, setting a new all-time record. The explosion of digital photography has since rendered such statistics almost unattractive. It was estimated that by 2015 according to the market research firm InfoTrends that global consumers will take more than one trillion digital photos. That's more than 12 times what was possible just 15 years earlier. But that only happens because Kyocera Corporation, a Japanese multinational ceramics and electronics manufacturer took the lead in 1999 to build a camera into a mobile phone leveraging the digital camera technology. What Kyocera did was to lead the invasion of the camera industry. An invasion that made cameras accessible to hundreds of millions of people all around the world and brought in a new era of possibilities.

This amazing possibility is the result of legendary inventor, Steven Sasson, a Kodak engineer whose work by the way was a threat to his company. Kodak surely understood that Sasson's invention was a clear tool of industry invasion. Their response demonstrated their competitive capacity and the reason for their being ousted eventually. It was a Kodak engineer who invented the digital camera. His company Kodak, understood the potential of digital technology in the camera industry. They knew it could put cameras into the hands of millions around the world and weaken their competitive position. So they thought to keep the invention away from everyone else. While they permitted him to keep working on it, his orders were to keep the idea away from everyone else.

Why did they do that? Kodak had an amazing control of 80% market share of the film and paper used for processing pictures. Digital camera thriving means the decline of their main source of revenue. Kodak therefore thought it was better to shut it down if possible.

But Kodak's decision was a dangerous one. Kodak was not trying to stop a piece of technology, they were trying to stop human advancement and happiness. Kodak was more concerned about protecting their business and existing technology than being excited about the chance to empower more people to share memories in the most convenient way. Kodak had lost sight of their calling in the industry which was what made them successful in the first instance.

Sustainable market leadership is not possible without a continuous effort to improve and increase value for your constituents. That requires a commitment to making your products and services obsolete by creating new ones and creating new ways of making them or delivering them. You need to understand that the world will continue to move forward and that means life will continue to improve and any person or group of persons that differentiate themselves and offerings in a way that resonate well with the buyers will have the respect of the market.

The implication of this is that the extent to which a market leader commits to advancing possibilities in their industry is the extent to which they can be relevant. The market leader who rather than commit to moving the industry forward decides to leverage whatever advantage it has to keep people limited by refusing to innovate and advance has created a moral ground for industry invasion. The market leader is out of position the day it chooses to place more value on profit than human beings, the world and its just systems.

Industry invasion is a well thought out, strategic effort designed to take over territories from a dominant player or players. The end result is the weakening of a strong player in some ways and loss of market share. So except when this will extend possibilities to more people and serve a greater good, this should be a last competitive option. There are other ways to compete successfully without destroying a rival's market or advantage.

But we live in a dog eat dog world and it's not different in business. Therefore, serving a market requires competence. Out performing your rivals is a demonstration of superior competence. As the market evolves, the out performing company must not only evolve but lead the evolution. A competitor's ability to change faster than the competitive environment is the only guarantee it will continue to lead the market. The bigger challenge is that when a market leader loses their leadership position, they usually not only lose the position of leadership in the industry but many times they are unable to compete at all.

The reason is that an authentic leader is one who has sentenced himself death already and everyday gives the organisation the opportunity to extend freedom to more and more people. With this understanding, the leading organisation feels a demand of destiny, a necessity and moral obligation to keep pushing the boundaries of possibilities. When the market leader abandons this course, ultimately because they forgot the philosophy behind the strategy that gave them their advantage, they also lose the moral competence to remain in business. The result is making wrong choices and myopic decisions that undermine the position of the company.

Such choices can include a decision to reduce the R and D budget or to underinvest in some of the company's critical assets. It might even be to invest in a technology they didn't have to. The effect of such decisions are hardly obvious as the balance sheet may continue to look good and the company lives on in past glory. By the time it is obvious, it is too late.

The major reason why it is difficult for most market leaders to keep their territory when invaded is because the invasion begins well before they even recognize it. When the signs of impending doom begin, the stock price still looks great, the profits are still great and nothing suggests a need to change anything. The company by focusing on its legacies and internal systems lose sight of the real changes taking place. By the time the changes begin to look like a problem most times, it's already late. In the years of the American cola wars, while the war intensified between CocaCola and Pepsi, CocaCola will not even mention Pepsi by name even though this competitor doubled its market share between the same period. While CocaCola was losing territory, it chose to act as though nothing was wrong and denying the obvious, obviously to give shareholders confidence but at the expense of losing market share.

The rule in competitive warfare is never to attempt defending an already lost territory. Many times many organisations ignore this rule. As stated elsewhere in the book, this among others defined the cause for which Nokia lost it and IBM remained. IBM knew when to stop fighting to keep a territory under attack, Nokia made that choice when it was too late.

In competitive warfare, the only justification for market leadership is your ability to provide superior value to all stakeholders. The reason is that suppliers will stay with you until they discover how to get more value elsewhere. Same goes for buyers and employees. Managers must reject as false the idea that it is possible to keep loyalty by deceit. That's an old idea which has been proven false multiple times. Keeping the truth from your stakeholders because it will threaten your position is a terrible mistake that could not only cost you your position but also a place in the industry.

Industry leadership is about taking the responsibility for industry growth. That means taking the responsibility for the increase of productivity in the industry. Productivity increases as all the stakeholders have the chance to increase efficiency. Taking the lead means committing to the ensuring superior value for every stakeholder. The rejection or ignorance of this idea weakens a company's ability to lead the market. Focusing on advancing your personal cause against the greater good disqualifies the company from leading the market and becomes a ground for a successful invasion of the industry.

Any organisation that chooses to prosper at the expense of the broader community, and a cause of social, environmental, and economic problems will be overthrown by another company with a more noble idea in the cause of time.

My hope in this chapter is to establish the moral condition for wagging a competitive invasion of an industry knowing that it comes at a cost and many times huge cost to the society. I understand positive-sum competition, where more than one company can be successful, a competition that expands the customers that are served, the needs that are met, and the overall value pool and I am a big advocate of that. Sometimes however, an industry leader must be taken out for the greater good of the society.

When a business begins to profit at the expense of the society, it's the responsibility of the people in that society to invade the industry and rid the organization of its power. That's exactly how it is in politics, it's the same in business. When a government makes a habit of abusing human rights and denying it's citizens freedom or treating a segment different from others it has established a moral and political ground for it's people to reject it. When the political suppression increases in magnitude leading to public outcry, then a moral ground is established for a foreign power to undermine the country's sovereignty and invade it.

Same is the true spirit of business. When a market leader for the purposes of protecting its own assets and advancing it's cause against public interest, anyone committed to the spirit of the vocation or industry should study the industry, design a plan and invade the industry. This is the spirit of innovation and progress through history and the power behind the rise of organizations like Google.

October 23, 2000 was the birth of the first ever self-serve online advertising platform – Google AdWords. By the end of their first year, Google ads had returned over $70 million. Google made $24.1 billion revenue for Q3 2018 from advertising. How did that happen? Well Google expanded possibilities for users.

While the traditional system offered pay per placement, rigid, company controlled advertising and no feedback, Google introduced pay per click or impression, flexible, self service and feedback mechanism. By redefining advertising in this way, they became an industry giant. Today, Alphabet, Google parent company is among the 100 best performing companies in the world ranking 13th. That's what happens when an organization understands market leadership, how to attain it and how to sustain it.

# BONUS CHAPTER

# THE SPIRIT OF STRATEGY

Strategy can only be as powerful as the spirit behind it. The lack of understanding of the spirit of strategy is the missing link for most managers who are unable to deliver on their strategy. According to a study by Marakon, less than 20% of even well-formulated strategies are executed successfully and, on average, firms deliver only 50% of the financial performance their strategies promise. That's why strategy is a serious issue because that's the foundation for superior performance.

That Apple makes high quality products is a fact that is well understood. Steve Jobs not only believes in quality but he's obsessed by it. In an interview he even insisted that it's not good enough to believe in quality products. Mr Jobs thinks companies have to approach the making quality products from a scientific point of view. This means understanding the reason behind making quality products. For most organizations this thinking is not well understood and even in cases where the most senior managers understand it, that understanding is usually a luxury everyone in the company can't enjoy.

But that's a very big mistake. Strategy defines a company's unique approach to competition. The motivation behind this approach is what I call spirit of the Strategy.

This spirit of strategy is what gives life to the strategy. The Organization that wins is the organisation in which everybody has a shared understanding of the motivation behind their approach to business.

You see, Apple didn't take a premium approach to competition for the fun of it or by a desire to make more money. The premium approach was rooted in the founder's obsession with quality. One wonders if this was why his exit from the company had it crumbling until they brought him back. I believe that Mr Jobs deep commitment to quality was the strength of the company and the keeper of their strategy.

Consider Mr. Job's advice to Mark Zuckerberg. In the early days of Facebook when it appeared they have hit the wall and many people were offering to buy Facebook, Mark Zuckerberg went to ask Steve Jobs for advice on what the right move should be. Steve Jobs simply emphasized on the need to reconnect with the mission of the company. He advised Mr Zuckerberg to set out time, break away from the noise to focus and gain clarity on the purpose of Facebook.

Mark travelled to India and for a month meditated and travelled through the country. Seeing how people connected, and having the opportunity to feel how much better the world could be if everyone has a strong ability to connect reinforced for him the importance of what they were doing at Facebook.

Mark returned from the trip, rejected all the offers for the company and committed to push on with his mission to "connect the world. The rest is history, Facebook is one of the most successful companies in the world. It was not just about a great strategy but a commitment to something bigger than monetary gains.

Cases have been written out of why legendary executive, Ron Johnson succeeded in setting up a very successful Apple Store but could not replicate the same in J C Penny. While there may be a lesson to learn about poor business analysis, ignoring advice from other people and a whole lot of other lessons, I think there is more importantly a lack of clarity about the spirit of J C Penny which every strategy must align with.

In an interview with Inc. Magazine, Ron Johnson recalled a time in the early days of setting up the Apple Store when he spoke up to Steve Jobs about something really bothering him on their way to a meeting. It was about how the store ought to be organized, a situation that will require a complete redesign of the Store. Mr Jobs initially resented this idea because he knew how expensive it was to redesign the store.

While at the meeting ten minutes later, Mr Jobs eventually got up and told everyone, "Well, Ron thinks our store is all wrong," Jobs said. "And he's right, so I'm going to leave now. And Ron, you work with the team and design the store."

Even though it would take longer to open the store because of the redesign, Jobs knew that it was worth taking the extra time to get it right. Why did Steve do this? Because he is connected to the Apple mission. That mission is the substance of their strategy, it is the spirit of the strategy. A commitment to the spirit of the strategy transforms the executive to a seeing executive, sharpens his/her discernment and creativity. But that's not all, the more connected the manager is to the essence of their strategy, the more his people will. When the manager slips into strategic inertia, everyone sleeps with him/her. This is usually the beginning of lousy performance.

The only reason why Ron Johnson was able to discern the right tactical approach here was because he understood ab initio the spirit of the strategy of Apple. It was his clarity about Mr Jobs obsession for quality that enabled him point out the tactical misstep in the Apple Store business strategy. This might have been what he missed in J C Penny where his concern for sleek and trend obscured his vision of who the J P Penny customer is and what will resonate with them. Mr Ron's intervention at J C Penny was a clear disaster. Mr Ron is a veteran executive, When he joined JC Penney in 2011, shareholders were so hopeful that everything will turn out right that the stock price of the company went up by 17%. But by 2012 instead of growth, sales last fell by 25 percent, resulting in a net loss of $985 million.

In an interview with Jim Aisner, Director, Media & PR at Harvard Business School, Harvard Business School marketing expert Rajiv Lal identified part of why JC Penney got into problem in the first place. According to Rajiv, JC Penney had lost their identity as there was no clear reason why someone would go there rather than all the other available options including Walmart and TJ Maxx. They lost their identity, but that didn't just happen, they first lost themselves. In other words they lost their essence, the spirit of their business approach, so they failed.

The first thing Mr Ron Johnson would have done was a rediscovery of this essence before enacting his three pillar strategy. You can't reposition a business suffering from strategic inertia without first waking them up to their original essence. When failing organisations reconnect with and recommit to the essence of their existence, the certainty of recovery is almost one hundred percent.

The case with IBM wasn't any different. With a 70% control of the information technology industry profits, the company was a clear industry leader. By 1990, they were the second most profitable company in the world. Between 1991 to 1993 however, the company lost nearly $16 billion.

How did this happen? First, computing moved away from the mainframe architecture (responsible for huge portions of IBM's revenue and profits) to the client/server model. Second, computers became commodity hardware with interoperable parts running interoperable technologies. This interoperability pushed prices lower, but IBM's managers could not break from their high-margin mainframe sales to compete in other areas.

Why did this happen? Why didn't IBM see what was coming and reposition themselves? It's not hard to know why. It is the spirit that lightens the path of the executive, it is also the spirit of the strategy that energizes the manager to do what must be done, take decisions that must be made and take the approach that must be taken.

The situation was turned around as a result of CEO Lou Gerstner's strategic insight. The information technology industry moved on and IBM stayed behind. Its core business in mainframes has died as a serious computing arena, and IBM is organizationally unsuited to compete in the PC market. Mr Lou knew they can't survive without building this strength. Sadly, they did not have the resources to build this capacity. In an interview with 30 days after his arrival at IBM, he stated that his concern was to "... get the fix done quickly in the company."

According to Thomas Watson Sr, who forged the disparate pieces of C-T-R into a strong, unified company that became IBM that, "It is the policy of this company never to be satisfied with what we have and always to anticipate the demands of the future." IBM had definitely lost touch with the essence of those words and reconnecting with those words was the power that will save IBM.

According to an article by D. Quinn Mills in the MIT Sloan Management Review, Lou Gerstner did not take IBM on a new course as much as he returned it to its roots. For decades, according to Mills, IBM had a strategy of supplying one-stop shopping for information services to large firms but the company strayed from that strategy in the 1980s, and as such confused and angered its customers, but has now returned to it. This was the major thing the new CEO did to turn the company around, it is reconnecting with it's spirit.

In the face of uncertainty and a fast changing business world therefore, a true commitment to the spirit of your strategy is the pathway to superior performance. Organizations that do this will survive and thrive, organisations that neglect this will regret it.

# →| Strategy Masterclass

## Why Strategy Masterclass?

### Global Perspectives ⇢→

TODAY'S ECONOMY TRANSCENDS GLOBAL BOUNDARIES AND CULTURAL REALITIES. OUR PROGRAMS BRING CURRENT GLOBAL BUSINESS PRACTICES FROM AROUND THE WORLD TO BEAR ON YOUR GOALS, YOUR

*picture insert - a session of Strategy Masterclass in Lagos, Nigeria.*

CAREER, AND YOUR ORGANIZATION. YOUR LEARNING IS ENHANCED BY OUR CONTINUOUS RESEARCH ON STRATEGY.

### Participant Mix ⇢→

THIS IS A DYNAMIC LEARNING ENVIRONMENT WHERE YOU AND A DIVERSE GROUP OF BUSINESS PEERS FROM A RANGE OF BACKGROUNDS, INDUSTRIES, AND COUNTRIES SHARE IDEAS AND DEVELOP AN ENLIGHTENED PERSPECTIVE ON THE ECONOMY, BUSINESS TRENDS, AND BEST PRACTICES.

### Overview

To thrive in today's highly competitive and rapidly evolving marketplace, executives must be able to craft and execute strategies that create lasting competitive Advantage.

Strategy Masterclass explores recent strategic moves by organisations globally and presents effective ways to identify and exploit opportunities, marshal and organize resources, and build and sustain a competitive advantage.

Immersed in a challenging curriculum that delves into the economics of competitive advantage, you will acquire the strategic tools to help your company build and maintain a leadership position.

Strategy Masterclass is a turbo-charged business growth clinic filled with practical insights for business effectiveness. It will help you elevate, escalate, and vastly expand your possibility paradigm --take-in the over-abundance of undiluted "private-client-grade" ideas, advice and strategies designed for forward-thinking executives.

It's designed for only 6 people maximum for two six-hour days working with Brian Reuben

Advisory team deeply, specifically, and multitudinously on their businesses' strategy, operations, and profit-boosting issues and opportunities.

It's 100% devoted to creating powerhouse outcomes, outstanding business strategies, and precise action plans to follow when you return back to your office. You will experience penetrating analysis, powerful recommendations and surprisingly detailed implementation instructions.

## Facilitation

Strategy Masterclass is based on the research and insights of Brian Reuben Advisory. The Masterclass is usually led by Dr. Brian Reuben.

Dr. Brian, widely acknowledged as an authority on the subject of Strategy is an Author, Advisor to business leaders, Keynote Speaker and an entrepreneur.

He is a featured speaker at business events in around the world and has trained and advised and mentored senior executives at several organizations globally

## Schedules

Strategy Masterclass holds monthly in Lagos - Nigeria, Dubai - UAE, Nairobi, Kenya and California - United States. For details on how to participate and charges kindly email admin@brianreuben.com

## Testimonials

*The Strategy Master Class is a practical approach to coming to terms with strategic realities of a competitive environment. The delivery method and the mix of backgrounds of participants in a close-up setting made the program all the more effective.*
JENNIS ANYANWU,
BUDGET AND PLANNING,
DEPARTMENT OF PETROLEUM RESOURCES, LAGOS.

*I have been restless since Strategy Masterclass ended. My understanding of strategy has been sufficiently challenged and I am in a hurry to implement this new knowledge. The opportunity for networking was also a plus. A great way to start the year! I recommend this masterclass to any executive looking to impact his industry while making a good return on their capital.*

ANITA AMORIGHOYE,
DIRECTOR, AYZER CENTER FOR ENTREPRENEURSHIP,
LAGOS

I BELIEVE THAT JESUS CHRIST IS THE SON OF GOD GIVEN FOR THE SALVATION OF THE WHOLE WORLD. I HAVE FAITH IN HIM AS MY LORD AND WISH TO SHARE SAME WITH YOU.

## *PRAYER OF SALVATION*

One of the smartest decisions you could ever make is to give your heart to Jesus Christ as the Lord of your life.

It's important you understand that Jesus actually came to this world, died for the sins of the whole world and was raised again for the justification of anyone who believes in him.

The bible said in Acts 4:12, 'Neither is there salvation in any other: for there is none other name under heaven given among men, whereby we must be saved.' There is no other name but the name of Jesus Christ of Nazareth.

If you are ready to give your heart to Jesus right now, pray this prayer with me from your spirit:

*Oh Lord God, I come to You, in the Name of Jesus. Your Word said that whosoever shall call on the name of Jesus shall be saved. I ask*

*Jesus to come into my heart and be the Lord of my life. I declare He is my Lord from this day hence forth. And according to Romans 10:9-10, I declare that I'm saved, I receive eternal life into my spirit. I'm born again. I now have Christ dwelling in me. Hallelujah.*

Congratulations and welcome to God's family,

Email brianreubenmentorship@gmail.com so we can send you important materials that will enhance your growth and walk with the Lord.

God bless you.

## ABOUT THE AUTHOR

Dr Brian Reuben is one of the most sought after thought leaders on the subject of Strategy in Africa.

Through his senior executive workshops he has helped position several businesses to produce remarkable results even in the most challenging and turbulent business environments.

Dr. Brian has trained and advised and mentored senior executives at several organizations globally. He is a featured speaker at business and leadership events around the world.

He has been interviewed and published in newspapers and television nationally and internationally on issues relating to leadership and strategy. His publications, radio and television programs has affected hundreds of millions of people all over the world.

He has written over 150 articles and facilitated over 200 strategy training programs for senior executives in diverse industries.

He sits on the board of a number of business and non-profit organisations around Africa

## OUR RIVETING RESOURCES

### WINE AND COFFEE MASTERMIND ALLIANCE

Extra-innovative, extraordinary, transformative mastermind alliance designed to deliver unparalleled business paradigm required to out-think, out-pace and out-perform your competition in unimaginable ways

The environment changes in multiple ways and faster than anyone can keep pace with. Your business decision and structures worth billions of dollars in time and money spent can be made obsolete even before your strategy is executed. This high level strategy assessment and review and business growth intensive program with Dr Brian Reuben will help you stay ahead of your industry causing the competition to respond to you rather than you responding.

## *STRATEGY AUDIT AND BUSINESS ASSESSMENT*

**Is your strategy up to date?** Are your people consistently making decisions in alignment with your choice of how and where to play in your industry? Are you clear on the actions of your competitors and the threats and opportunities they bring to you? Are you likely under-utilizing the unique opportunities you have to make money posing as roadblocks for you?

Keep your strategy upto date, transform you business approach, improve your positioning and discover amazing new ways to unlock more value from your assets and investments.

This extraordinary business assessment exercise take place at your own boardroom with you and your team as Dr Brian leads the conversation analysing your industry and all related industries, examining and reexamining rivaries actions to see beyond the obvious to uncover intentions. Analysing recent policies, substitutes to your products and services PLUS hidden preeminent ways of shaping and restructuring your industry in order to gain uncommon advantage.

Dr Brian charges upto $1000 to answer one business question. His advice has saved several business executives millions in time and money and accelerated business growth for decision makers in diverse industries.

STRATEGY AUDIT AND BUSINESS ASSESSMENT program affords you the rare chance to have a fine breed consultant bring his amazing insights and experience to bear on your business given you unquestionable advantage.

Understand that investing in 'general' training programs can't give you the highest and greatest value in terms of time, energy and opportunity cost. You need 'case-specific' answers, solutions, strategies and ingenious ideas that have worked wonders and produced amazing results for Dr. Brian's clients who pay upto $10000 per day to have him work with them on an exclusive basis.

To invest in this opportunity now email admin@brianreuben.com

For more information kindly contact Brian Reuben International Office admin@brianreuben.com